Overalls to Pinstripes
An Autobiography

Ray Barrett

PublishAmerica
Baltimore

ISBN: 1-4241-8115-1
PUBLISHED BY PUBLISHAMERICA, LLLP
www.publishamerica.com
Baltimore

Printed in the United States of America

This autobiography is dedicated to my family and grandchildren. As defined in a song I wrote, "Real Love" in a family is found in a baby's smile, and grandchildren.

Acknowledgments

I wish to express my sincere appreciation to the following for their assistance in the development of this manuscript: my niece, Gaylyn Bell, who dedicated time and effort in typing my difficult-to-read writing; my daughter, Michelle Hancock, who helped me make this possible; and my loving wife, Marilyn, who protected the typed title page, in an old antique typewriter, for ten years, waiting for "The Rest of the Story."

Foreword

When I was a young man trying to find my way, I had no plans laid out or understanding of what I hoped to accomplish. I had no tangible assets, no money, very little education and at that time, no entrepreneurial thoughts or talent. I just tried to get by. Fortunately or unfortunately, whichever way one might view my situation, no one ever offered to assist me or provide any guidance.

As I matured into adulthood, it became clear what I did not want to do and what I needed to do to get on a career path. I took advantage of an opportunity to do this by going to college on the G. I. Bill.

Fortunately, as I struggled to succeed and complete college, opportunities began to become evident and available. The rest, as they say, is history. I was fortunate in my profession to have capable and credible people around me. I assisted them and they assisted me. I gained substantially both financial and management knowledge from these professional relationships.

Hopefully, this personal history and my suggestions on professional growth will be of benefit and provide insight on how one might go from basically nothing to a financially independent career and retirement.

Chapter 1
Early Years

I don't remember my early childhood years. For me, it seems I woke up and found myself in the first years of school. I understand my early childhood years were quite difficult. My dad died when I was three and my brother was a baby. This was during the Depression period and making a living or just getting by was extremely difficult. My mother was quite young and could not provide for two small children. An orphanage was considered and almost became a reality.

There was discussion during this period after my dad's death to place us with one of the grandparents, if they would take us. When I was about four or five (not sure when), we went to live with my mother's side of the family, so she could find work and try to provide for us. I have never inquired into the details of the what, where, why and when of the situation. I simply accepted it. All I know is we were taken in by my mother's parents in lieu of the orphanage and this would now be basically our foster home.

My grandfather (Papa) and grandmother (Mama) lived on a farm near Packton, Louisiana. This was near where I was born in Georgetown, Louisiana. Papa drove the school bus, which required a before-daylight get-up-and-get-ready for the twenty miles to school each weekday. There were still three of Mama and Papa's eight children living at home when my brother and I became part of the family.

During my can't-remember young childhood years, I do remember Papa built a new house. As I recall, it was larger than the previous house. As we moved into the new house, my brother and I were given a bed in the same room with Papa. We shared this room and bed until I left home at the age of eighteen, though other rooms were available.

Also during this period, there was no electricity or gas for lighting and/or heating. Water came from a well and the bathroom was an outhouse. The outhouse was a nice one with two holes. I often wondered why, because no one shared it. Taking a bath meant getting into a washtub maybe twice a week, with warm water heated on the wood cook stove during the wintertime. Our summer baths consisted of bathing outside by the well house using cold well water from a bucket, or taking a dip in the pond. At the time I thought these methods were more than adequate and I guess they were.

Our light came from kerosene (coal oil) lamps and heat was from the fireplace in Mama's bedroom, and our wood cook stove. It was pretty crowded in Mama's bedroom at nights during the winter months. As you can imagine, it was hot in the summer and cold in the winter.

During this period, my brother and I were basically accepted as members of the family and treated somewhat the same as the other family members. There was, however, always that feeling and reflective understanding that we were not members of the family and should understand that we were fortunate to be there. As I became older, I began to understand we were not part of the immediate family, but was grateful we had a place to live.

There were many things, even today, I think about during my years of growing up out on the old farm. Each fall and winter required we hunt for meat. This consisted of squirrels, deer and wild hogs. This was the mainstay of our meat for the year. Deer was the replacement for beef. Fortunately, there were numerous deer and wild hogs, which were hunted, killed, butchered and placed in the smokehouse. One of my chores was to keep hickory logs on the fire. A fire in the smokehouse continued for in excess of a month. This meat was salted down and smoke cured and eaten for the rest of the year.

I received my first real gun, a single-shot .22-caliber rifle, when I was about seven years old. An old gentleman who stayed with my Great Aunt Molly also gave me a 16-gauge shotgun that same year. I thought the gods had really smiled on me. I still have both guns. It is really interesting to note with all the requirements and concerns about guns and gun control today that when I was a child and until I left the farm, a fully loaded accessible rifle sat in basically every corner in the house. We knew not to bother these guns.

The old home place

Me 1940

My playground

Mother, brother, and me

There is no way I can recall the number of squirrels, deer, wild hogs, goats and other animals and birds I have shot and killed primarily for food during my years on the farm. As a result, I have no desire to hunt deer or anything else today.

In the early spring, plowing with a mule began and crops and a garden were planted. This consisted of corn, Irish and sweet potatoes, tomatoes, watermelons, cantaloupe, various other vegetables, cotton, peanuts and sugarcane. I've probably left some plantings out, but I thought at the time we planted everything that would grow, including weeds. The planting later meant working in the fields and garden chopping weeds and grass with a hoe, following a mule and plowing all day long. In the middle of summer in a corn patch, with ninety percent humidity, it was pure torture. A dip in the pond at the end of the day was the only relief I could look forward to. I often wondered why we planted corn to feed the mules we used to plant the corn. Why not get rid of the mules?? However, they were used for other things, i.e., planting the garden and dragging the hogs that we had killed out of the woods.

Every year it was necessary to cut trees with a two-man crosscut saw for firewood, split the wood and gather pine knots to start the fires in the fireplace and wood stove. The greatest hazards were rattlesnakes and coral snakes. There was no shortage of snakes. I've come very close many times, but have never been bitten by one.

Each fall, the sugar cane was made into syrup using the mules and an old Ford motor to grind juice from the cane. This was always a remembered annual event. People would come from miles around to watch Papa make syrup. It is enjoyable recalling these times when, as I got older, sips of "white lightning" (whiskey from distilling sugar cane, i. e. syrup skimming) became available. It was interesting to watch the birds, cows and hogs become intoxicated from eating and drinking fermented cane mashing. What I would have given for a video camera back then.

I can recall on numerous occasions the home place becoming an island. Flooding from creeks and small streams would cover all the land around the house, completely wiping out the crops in the fields and fences. When the water receded, we would fix the fences and start over replanting. There is a situation I remember and at the time, I thought was a proper test. Papa, with his responsibility as a school bus driver, tried to never miss a day of school. There were times the bridge near our house would be engulfed by high water. He would stop the bus, walk out on the wooden boards of the bridge, literally bobbing up and down from the water, jump up and down several times in several places, and since the bridge held him with no problem, he would come back and drive the school bus across the "breathing" bridge. It must have worked because it allowed us to safely cross the bridge every time.

Good times for a boy like me in the country included swimming in the creek and pond after we chased the snakes out, or fishing in these same water holes. Picking grapes and making homemade wine was also another good time, until we got caught. I can still taste the cold well water.

My grandmother was a very religious woman, a Pentecostal. I sometimes went to church with her. Papa would drive her to church in the school bus, but he never went in the church. He waited outside for her until church was over. I have seen things occur in that church that defy my understanding or explanation, such as people fainting, speaking a language that I could not understand and seeing Mama (who was a very large woman) jump up and dance around on legs she could hardly walk on when not in church. The next day, she would be unable to walk again. To this day, I cannot explain what was occurring or why.

It was interesting to see the talent that was demonstrated. Some of the church members, in some cases the entire family, played the guitar, mandolin, banjo, piano and other instruments and sang better than the professionals of today. They were good. A lot of the songs I know and play today came from that little ol' Pentecostal church.

My schoolhouse in Georgetown was a three-story building. Every class in school went to this building. The third floor was the auditorium, equipped with a fire escape which happened to be a large three- to four-foot-diameter tube or pipe which opened at the top and discharged at ground level. This was quite a slide and was used quite frequently, even though it meant punishment in the form of paddling. There was nothing else anywhere that was equivalent to this slide. You could, without any restrictions, be traveling fifteen to twenty miles per hour when you hit the bottom opening. The landing was pretty rough. However, someone was always putting oil or grease in it, which resulted in quite a mess on the clothes. As I stated, every grade level was in this one building. I remember having to combine all the boys and girls from the ninth to twelfth grades to get enough of each to make a basketball or softball team. In my grade school, I seldom wore shoes to school during the warm months, and overalls were the basic clothing (secondhand, of course). About half the kids in school were in the same category as me, just plain poor. Lunch consisted of a couple of biscuits and jelly, with pork or venison, in a brown paper bag with my name on it.

I guess we did learn a little from our school days; I could read and write and knew a little math and chemistry. It was enough to get me started. The sports were the driving force to keep me in school. I couldn't wait to get my basketball uniform, warm-up jacket and pants. I felt I had arrived when I made the team. I also always looked forward to softball and track. However, we didn't have uniforms for those sports. In my third year of high school, a gymnasium was built which really made everything great. Up to this time, all basketball games at our school were played outside in the heat and dust on a dirt court. We had one principal, one teacher per class and no administrative people, other than a janitor. The teachers also substituted for coaches in our athletics. Our chemistry teacher was the track coach and our history teacher was the basketball coach. It seemed everyone doubled up. There were many things that occurred during my school years; however, getting some amount of education just happened, as it was low on my list of priorities.

In my final year of high school, a major event occurred. Rural electrical power became a reality. Mama and Papa got electricity, which now allowed water well pumps to be installed for indoor plumbing (no more outhouse) as well as electric lights. Heating was still done by the fireplace and wood stove, but at least we could see at night.

Two days after my high school graduation, I left the farm with my sparse wardrobe and no money, to go to work for an oil exploration company located in New Orleans where my mother lived. I didn't see my mother too much when I was with Mama and Papa. She would come visit two or three times a year and give Mama money for them to use. Birthdays, as we know them today, were not celebrated or any attention given them. As a child or teenager, I never had a birthday party or present. At that time, I did not know people celebrated birthdays.

I would save some of the money I earned helping my uncle and catch a bus or train to go visit Mother during the summer months. Even after Mother remarried, there was no mention of my brother and me going to live with her. I have often wondered why.

I was glad to leave the farm and get started on my own. I had no money and did not have to worry about taking anything with me as there was nothing to take. Mother knew a family in New Orleans, whom I had met, and they arranged the job "opportunity(??)" for me. At this time, Mother had gone to school to become a beautician, had remarried and now operated a beauty shop on Royal Street. I was now beginning to understand what getting out on my own was all about. Within two days after my high school graduation, I was employed and out in the marshes of Louisiana.

Chapter 2
Beginning Employment

At eighteen years of age, my first taste of employment was a lasting experience. During this period (1950), jobs were hard to find and I was glad to have one. The job required I work the Gulf coastline of Louisiana, Mississippi and Texas in the lakes, swamps, marshes and Gulf of Mexico. It was a job which required ten days living on a "quarter" (house) boat and four days back in civilization. The job was initially pure torture. Each day, hot or cold, rain or shine, we wore the same wet, mud-coated clothes and shoes, which had been rinsed in the bayou the previous night. Weather, other than a hurricane, was not a deterrent to the job. My first assignment was on a drilling crew. This consisted of a marsh buggy or boat taking us to the drilling site, pulling or pushing a small drilling barge. The drilling apparatus consisted of a triangular upright piping system which attached to a stand on the edge of the barge to hold a ten-foot drill pipe. A water pump was connected to the pipe and it took two people with large pipe wrenches to turn the drill pipe. I was on one end of these wrenches. Fortunately, the marsh was soft and for about twenty to thirty feet of the eighty to one hundred feet we drilled, the drilling was easy; the other sixty to seventy feet was another story. The average work day was about ten hours, depending on progress made each day.

It became obvious to me, with the muck, snakes, alligators and mosquitoes, this was not a career-type job. During a typical day, as many as fifty to one hundred snakes could be seen, and at nightfall the only survival from mosquitoes was to immerse yourself in the water with a cap over your nose for breathing. About dusk, you could hear them beginning to buzz, literally a roar. They would fill the air. A person could not survive a night exposed in the marshes. Fortunately, they were not bad during the day. You prayed each night for the boat to be on time.

Finally, after about six months of being up to my neck in the marsh mud, I was transferred to a survey crew. The surveyor, who was also quite young, and I became good friends. During the next six months, he taught and I learned how to run a transit (survey instrument) and how to do the surveying required by the oil exploration company. I was promoted to another quarter boat and given my own boat and survey crew. At the age of nineteen, I became the youngest surveyor the company (General Geophysical) had ever had. Life was much better now. I could choose my work hours and had my designated boat, marsh buggy, airboat and helicopter to conduct my survey responsibilities, depending on the conditions and terrain involved. All I had to do was stay ahead of the drill and jug line crews. I identified where the holes were to be drilled and where the seismometers (jugs) were to be located. This operation was called "Doodle Bugging," which tests for oil and gas beneath the earth's surface of the ground, marsh or underwater, twenty-five to fifty feet apart in

a straight line for about a quarter mile. The cable is hooked to a chart recording station where each jug is recorded separately. An explosive charge (generally one hundred pounds of ammonium nitrate in one-pound cans screwed together) is pushed down to the bottom of each drill hole. The explosive is detonated one hole at a time and the vibrations in the earth picked up by the jugs are recorded. The effect of the underground explosion is somewhat the same as seismometers used in measuring an earthquake. A cross grid of a specific area is mapped with explosions and jugs and the sub terrain is analyzed for pockets of oil and gas that might be in that area.

General Geophysical Company, 1950-1953, Quarters boat

It's a hit-or-miss-type gamble. If a potential for oil and gas was located and identified, I also had the responsibility to identify and mark where the oil or gas well was to be located.

As one might surmise, this type of activity could create many unexpected events that leave a lasting memory. Some of these memorable moments are noted.

I have seen the explosive charges (one hundred pounds) that were thought to be one hundred feet underground float back to the surface of the drill pipe. The one-pound cans of explosives are screwed together, and wooden poles, hooking together, are used to push the string of cans (explosives) deep down, to bottom of the drill pipe. When detonated, pieces of the drill pipe and the push poles are blown into the air like arrows in flight, and mud and marsh blown over a quarter mile away, in some cases injuring people on the jug line.

In another situation, while surveying in wide open water, I warned the jug crew of a developing fog out in the Gulf. I told the supervisor to shut down and get out of the area while he could do so. They did not heed my warning and became lost in the fog. Two people and four airboats were lost due to developing rough weather. The fog prevented the crew from knowing which direction to take to get to the quarter boat. We found the crew (approximately ten people) the next morning in one boat. Unfortunately, two people were never found. These were flat-bottom airboats which could not withstand the huge waves.

I also experienced a young man falling overboard near a docked boat by the quarter boat and disappearing. Everyone expected him to surface and be okay. We found him drowned under the boat sometime later, clinging to the propeller. We assume he got under the boat and for some reason, could not get out. We had difficulty pulling him loose.

In another situation, a turtle, weighing approximately eight hundred pounds and six feet in diameter, became entangled in the jug line. We were in about six to eight feet of clear water. Unfortunately, the turtle had to be destroyed. This was done by dropping one-pound cans of explosives on him and detonating the explosives. It looked like a destroyer dropping depth charges on a submarine. It took a couple of hours to stop the turtle. The jug line had to be replaced. The turtle was winched onto the back of a shrimp boat and sold to a soup factory in Venice, Louisiana, for approximately four hundred dollars. The crew split the proceeds which amounted to about twenty to thirty dollars each. That was good money back then.

With no land in sight, my crew and I were laying a line in about four feet of water when the poor guy on the tail of the survey chain (two hundred feet) began yelling that a snake was after him. He immediately became a wave runner and sure enough, when he came close to me, there was a snake about twenty feet behind him, swimming as fast as he could in order to catch his prey. When the snake saw me, he decided I was easier prey. I hit the snake with one of the wooden stakes we were using. He immediately went into the attack mode. The next hit ended his career. It was a rattlesnake with thirteen rattles. He was looking for an object to crawl upon just to get out of the water.

We were never removed from the marshes for an approaching hurricane. At that time, we were fortunate if we knew one was coming. There were no radios or television. I experienced only two minimum hurricanes while working in the marshes. One broke our explosives barge loose from its mooring and came within a few feet of our quarter boat. It was quite a battle to get that barge out of the marsh.

Marsh Buggies and Drilling Barge, Golden Meadow, Louisiana. Me on a tripod surveying in the Gulf, 1950-1953

After one storm I recovered a dragline on a barge, floating free some thirty miles out in the Gulf of Mexico. Although I was, by maritime standards, now owner of the barge and its contents (the dragline), I returned them to their rightful owner. The company received a good payment of gratitude from the owners of the dragline.

I had occasions when the tripod (about thirty feet in length) which held my survey instrument would turn over in the rough water. In order to save the transit, I would unscrew it while the tripod was falling and place the transit, which weighed about ten pounds, on my head and tread water, without a life preserver, until the boat came and picked me up. This could be for a few minutes to half an hour, depending on where the boat was located. The tripod always had a life preserver to mark where it was. Needless to say, I had to stay in good shape to save the transit.

It was standard procedure on my survey crew to drag a small boat (pirogue) with a small steel cable two hundred feet behind the marsh buggy. A stake was placed every two hundred feet marking the survey line.

One time, the helicopter that was delivering me to the survey crew landed between the marsh buggy and the small boat. Unknown to the pilot and everyone else involved, the pontoons on the helicopter went under the small cable, which was hidden by the marsh grass. When the helicopter pilot decided to take off, he and everyone else realized a major mistake had occurred—the helicopter dragged the small cable and boat about ten feet into the air and the helicopter propellers threw mud and grass about one hundred feet in all directions. The helicopter was flipped onto its back. Fortunately, no one was hurt and we removed the helicopter over a two-day period by barge pulled by a marsh buggy to a boat. It was a remarkable and frightening sight to witness.

My work in the marshes and Gulf had some benefit. Not only was I in excellent condition, but I also was able to save some money. It was during my first year at work that I accrued enough money (several hundred dollars) to purchase my first car, a used 1949 Ford. I thought I was now "picking in high cotton." I had attained a degree of freedom I had always thought about.

When my draft notice came in 1953, drafting me into the U.S. Army (Korean Conflict), it was a worry and a blessing. I was being removed from the marshes, but now may be going into a war. I wasn't sure which one was the blessing.

Me at home place with my car

Chapter 3
U.S. Army

I was drafted into the U.S. Army in November 1953. I reported to New Orleans and that same day, I was put on a train and sent to San Antonio, Texas. After a couple of days in San Antonio (Fort Sam Houston), I was sent by airplane to Ft. Belvoir, Alexandria, Virginia, near Washington, D.C. We received our uniforms and other gear upon arrival in San Antonio. The Ft. Belvoir facility near Washington, D.C., was a Corps of Engineers training center. It was in Ft. Belvoir I received all my basic training, i.e., building bridges, laying out and dismantling mine fields, booby traps and other special-mission-type operations.

My platoon leader was a "Pathfinder." This is a special U.S. Army group, highly trained in survival, with approximately two hundred members. Their role was to be dropped behind enemy lines and determine where the rest of the troops should be deployed. Theirs was not a very good survival rate and my platoon leader was pretty banged and shot up. For some reason, he liked me and because, I assume, I was in such excellent physical condition from working in the marshes, he tried to get me to become a Pathfinder. I politely advised "no thanks," but thanks for asking. It also meant two more years of service. He still gave me special training relative to his professional experience while at Ft. Belvoir. He had the capability of killing someone with his bare hands in less than a few seconds. Although he was someone you did not want to mess with, I enjoyed and gained beneficial training while associated with this special individual.

Fortunately, the Korean Conflict was about to end and I was not required for overseas duty. My tenure with the army consisted of basic training and attending Cartographic Drafting (map drawing) School at Ft. Belvoir, Virginia, for about six months. I was then sent to Camp McCoy, Wisconsin, as the post surveyor and supervisor to repair roads and bridges. This was during the summer months and the weather was excellent. The post was basically used for training the reserve units and National Guard. Only a few (fifty to one hundred) permanent people were on the post, except during summer months. This was good duty.

After Camp McCoy, I was transferred to Ft. Riley, Kansas. This was not a good place to be anytime of the year. While at Ft. Riley, I met an individual with whom I became friends. Later, he was a groomsman in my wedding. He played first base for the post baseball team. I went to a couple of practice sessions with him and happened to see some of the post softball players practicing. I knew I was a better pitcher than these individuals and asked if I could try out for the team. My last eight months of service was Ft. Riley's softball fast-speed pitcher. We played college teams and other army post teams. Being on the post softball team was good duty. Unfortunately, it was during this time, while playing basketball, I damaged my knee. I am suffering today for my actions some fifty years ago.

While at Ft. Riley, there was one situation that could have had a major effect on my life. While driving in my car around the far corners of the base, I found base personnel digging large holes and burying dump-truck loads of clothing and tools into these holes. Needless to say, I took advantage of this and without permission, removed clothing and tools from the dug holes to give to my family in Louisiana. My car was loaded down with blankets, coats, tools and other things. Unfortunately, a routine search of privately owned cars was conducted before I could leave and I was told to report to the division commander. I explained what I had stumbled upon. He was obviously aware of the disposal of these perfectly good materials. His instructions were: Take the things you have to your home. I will not hold you responsible and strongly suggest you do not tell anyone about what you saw or how you obtained these items. I later learned this disposal inventory was an annual event conducted to get new replacement materials and clothing, for example, replacing the new with new. What a waste. I do not know if the practice continued. I didn't want to know and did not mention anything about it while I was in the service. We still have some of the blankets.

Me at Ft. Riley, Kansas

The two-year tenure in the army provided me the opportunity to go to college on the G.I. Bill. I made the decision not to return to my previous job of working in the marshes and to enter Louisiana State University in Baton Rouge, Louisiana. I was now approximately five years out of high school and anything I might have learned in school had long been forgotten.

Chapter 4
College

The first year at LSU was a learning experience. I basically had to start over with everything, especially math and chemistry. Fortunately, the university was tolerant with Korean veterans and I was allowed to slowly gain from the refresher courses. In making a decision on what I wanted to pursue, I asked which degree, other than being a doctor or lawyer, paid the most upon graduation. At that time, chemical engineering was, and still is today, one of the highest paid degrees and/or professions one can enter. It is also one of the most difficult degrees one could attain, but was also one of the most versatile and in-demand professions one can enter. I decided, "That's what I'll be," a chemical engineer. However, no one until later advised me on what was required to become a chemical engineer. It required extensive math, chemistry and part of every other engineer curriculum, i.e., electrical, mechanical, industrial, etc., available, adding up to over 160 hours (four and one-half years) to graduate. Regardless of this, I stepped into the river and started to swim. After my first year, I was advised by counselors that I should try something else, perhaps agriculture. They were convinced I did not have what was necessary to become a chemical engineer or any other type of engineer. I believed for a while that they might be right. On the other hand, they gave me an incentive to press on and the attitude "I'll show you."

In my second year of college, when I finally began to take chemical engineering courses, the first class I attended was composed of roughly fifty students. The professor advised us that out of a class of fifty, approximately ten would graduate. It really gave me a comforting feeling of how easy it was going to be. I might add, nine of the fifty graduated. The rest failed or quit.

During my first year of college, another very important event occurred. I met and married Marilyn Dark. I met Marilyn at a basketball practice session at Winnfield High School. She was filling in for her friend, the girls' basketball coach. I had brought a young lady I was dating to the practice session. I asked Marilyn for a date. She refused. I called again the next day, another refusal. Each time, "no thanks." After several days, I tried again for what was to be the last time and she accepted. Later, I found out she was running references on me. I have no idea how she obtained a favorable reference.

On our first date, I was helping a friend of mine brand and "dehorn" some cows. I will not describe this event and only say that I was run over by one of the cows. Needless to say, I was pretty roughed up for our first date and late, which did not go over too well.

Anyway, even though I had absolutely nothing to offer, after several months of dating, we were married, even though her family advised against it. She took a big gamble. She was a valuable asset in helping me make it through college. Marilyn worked for the secretary of state of Louisiana and somehow, we made it financially. After fifty years of marriage and things now considerably financially different, we have a great family and six grandchildren. I'm glad my references checked out and that I didn't give up.

After several close calls toward failing out, I finally caught on to the chemical engineering curriculum and got my degree in February 1959, with not-too-bad grades. Some summers during this period, I took courses and worked for my previous company, surveying and locating oil/gas drilling sites in places like Seminole, Texas, and Rayne, Louisiana.

One summer toward my senior year, I took summer classes and also worked for Allied Chemical Solvay Division in Baton Rouge, Louisiana. We made soda ash and caustic soda. It was a run-down plant which should have been closed. It made me wonder if chemical engineering was going to be like this. I received a job offer from this company upon graduation.

I also taught a survey lab in the civil engineering department at LSU. During a few weeks each summer, I worked with a civil engineer professor laying out subdivisions in the Baton Rouge area and in South Louisiana. These professors treated me very well.

I also spent about a week with a civil engineer professor (Dr. Dantien) at his home in Golden Meadow, Louisiana. We were there to lay out a subdivision outside the town. You don't get any more Cajun than Golden Meadow. His parents, where we stayed, did not speak English (only broken French). I found this quite interesting and an experience on how the real Cajuns live. They were what I call genuine people. It was a totally different world than North Louisiana.

Fortunately, the head of the chemical engineering department, Dr. Jesse Coates, who is well known in the industry, seemed to like me (possibly because I was a veteran) and took me under his wing. This became an asset upon graduation. The job market was in a recession with few jobs available. As a direct result of Dr. Coates' recommendations, I received two job offers, neither of which was very desirable. One job was in a carbon black plant and the other a steel mill. In hindsight, maybe he didn't like me the way I thought he did. I decided to take an offer of $425 per month with Thiokol Chemical Corporation. This company was building a major plant in Brigham City, Utah, to manufacture a solid-propellant intercontinental ballistic missile (ICBM) called the "Minuteman" for the Air Force.

This was a long way from home, but it provided me an opportunity to get in on the ground floor and develop and/or work on something no one had ever done before. I considered it an excellent opportunity. It turned out to be as I expected—dangerous and rewarding.

Chapter 5
Professional Work History

Thiokol Chemical Corporation
Brigham City, Utah
Manager, Specialty Operations, Wasatch Division

We arrived in Brigham City in February 1959. Snow was everywhere and the Mormons were everywhere. It took some adapting to both the climate and the people. We purchased our first home using the G.I. Bill, which allowed the purchase with no money down. The home was newly constructed, very small and cost $12,000.

I was the approximate three hundredth employee at the new site, which, five years later would grow to over eight thousand employees.

My first and immediate supervisor at Thiokol was an older man named Paul, who had previously been an executive with General Electric. Due to alcoholism, he was released by General Electric. I learned a lot from Paul on how to work with other people. I once gave him a report I was assigned to prepare. He asked me a question relating to the contents to which I could not give him a definitive answer. Without saying a word, he threw the report in the wastebasket and advised me to never prepare another report of any kind unless I know everything about the report. I provided Paul numerous other reports after that, but he never asked me another question, as he knew I was well prepared to answer.

My work experience in the chemical engineering profession began immediately. I became the responsible process engineer for the development of the new solid-propellant fuel and the manufacture of the first-stage rocket of the Minuteman ICBM, including the development, construction and installation of the manufacturing facilities. Although highly dangerous, it was a job that I enjoyed. Approximately one year later, the first stage of the

Minuteman, under my development and supervision, was ready for a static test. This involved putting the "head" of the missile against the mountain, locking it down and firing. My first test, which I thought would be successful, lasted less than 0. 3 of a second and lighted the entire side of the mountain with scattered burning pieces. We learned very quickly that this was not a material or process that could be taken lightly. Basically, it was an explosive that required very little to get it excited.

Two to three years later, we were firing the first-stage Minuteman with over ninety-eight percent success rate using fuel formulas I developed and cast into a casing shell (fifty-six-inch-diameter tube) that was so thin one could literally stick a ballpoint pen through it. All of this was under U.S. Air Force contract. When development was complete, the operating procedures and processes were given to the Air Force. They converted these secret documents into "highly secret" Air Force documents. I decided I would like one of these documents, which had my name as the engineer. Upon request of the document, which bore my name as engineer, I was refused because I was cleared "secret," but not for "top secret." My development and manufacturing report had made it to the highest secret classification.

A first-stage Minuteman motor is lifted out of a large outdoor heat- and vacuum-controlled processing pit for propellant casting and curing.

Both horizontal and vertical static test firings of first-stage Minuteman were conducted. This is a vertical test.

After four years, I was asked to build and manage a new developmental plant called High Energy Pilot Plant. I accepted this assignment. It became obvious this was a new adventure as the plant was constructed over five miles from the main plant. In this plant, absolute discipline and responsibility were required. Only cotton clothing could be worn and every solid item and tool had to be accounted for at all times. All oxidizer materials were placed underground in the event of lightning, which occurred quite frequently, because static electricity in the area could set off an explosion. The main new oxidizer, which I will not name, was, as one might understand, quite sensitive. For example, one employee failed to shower and wash properly before going home. Once home, he decided to clean under his nails. His finger was blown off by a small amount of this propellant. Another employee gave a small twist to empty an in-line sediment glass and the condensed crystals exploded, removing part of his hand.

On only one occasion did I knowingly come close to an accident. I had left the building and was approximately fifty feet away when the building blew up, throwing me about fifteen feet into a bunker. Fortunately, I was not hurt. However, this made me realize that it could only be a matter of time in a careless moment or unexpected incident, when my time would be up. Although all operations were conducted remotely, each time a problem occurred, someone had to go into the building and fix the problem. I always went with a volunteer (generally a reluctant volunteer) to resolve the problem. This began to weigh on me, especially after we had our son, Michael. After two years of managing this operation, I began considering other opportunities.

After numerous years of trying to have a child, we decided to adopt a baby. In November 1964, we received our first child, a boy born in Boise, Idaho, on September 11, 1964, and named him James Michael. It was truly a blessing.

Utah was a good place for us. The climate was not bad. There were four distinct seasons, with winter being the most recognizable. Snow occurred quite often, especially in the mountains. It was a great outdoor area and I spent a great deal of time hunting and fishing. My hunting buddies were Jim White and Jerry Mason. Jerry became head (manager) of all Thiokol operations a few years after I left. He retired from this position following the *Challenger* disaster. Unfortunately, he made the decision to "go" after the questionable freeze in Florida. In 2004, I learned of his death, which occurred on a hunting trip. I was told he was found dead, probably of a heart attack; although at eighty years of age, he was in excellent condition.

I have fond memories of Jerry and our hunting/fishing trips. Once, we decided to hike into Yellowstone and camp on a small lake, taking only fishing gear, apples and potatoes (to live off the land). After about a ten-mile hike and setting up our tents, we decided to catch some fish to eat. Within two hours and no fish, all our fishing tackle was broken by larger-than-expected fish and we realized it was apples and potatoes for dinner. We hiked back out after dark and returned home never to intentionally live off the land again.

Another interesting trip involved boating thirty miles down the Green River to a point where the Green River and the Colorado River meet. Some sixty to seventy boats were involved in this adventure. The Green River was very shallow in places, with numerous rocks that did not like motorboat propellers. All boats were to stop some fifteen to twenty miles downstream. This is where we were supposed to spend the night, eat steaks, gas up and continue the next day. There were two major problems at the stopping point: (1) There was no place for sixty to seventy boats to tie up on the steep banks, and (2) the gas was provided through a hose with no valve from a tanker truck on a bluff some one hundred to one hundred fifty feet above the landing area. The boats were tied to each other and formed a bridge to get to shore. All night long, the lead boat would break loose and ten to twenty boats had to be chased down with another boat and retied. Gasoline came out of the hose about twenty gallons per minute, all over the ground and everywhere. It reminded me of the Keystone Cops movies. Everyone who filled their tanks went straight to the river to wash off the gas. Fortunately, no one was badly hurt. We finally made it after going through about four propellers and a small hole in the boat and being dead tired. It seemed we had a way of choosing really "fun" trips.

There were numerous other situations from which another book could probably be written. Both are now gone, but I will always cherish the time Jerry, Jim and I spent together.

While in Utah, we had the opportunity to see a lot of the West, including trips into Yellowstone in the winter on large snowmobiles. It was really beautiful. We also had numerous visitors, each wanting to go to Yellowstone. At that time, one could visit Yellowstone National Park or the Grand Tetons without any difficulty or necessity of a reservation.

We still have good friends in Brigham City, Utah. It was a place to which you truly could return.

Texas Instruments, Inc.
Dallas, Texas
Manager, Chemical Handling and Processing

Some friends of ours, whom we had known for several years in Utah (Marilyn's boss), had moved from Utah to Dallas, the headquarters of Texas Instruments (T.I.). He was in their human resources group and called us on several occasions to come to work at Texas Instruments. In 1965, I accepted an offer to become manager of Texas Instruments Chemicals, handling the procurement and processing division in Dallas, Texas.

To our surprise, after years of trying and upon our arrival in Dallas, we found out that Marilyn had finally become pregnant. She became pregnant shortly after our arrival in Dallas and unfortunately, it occurred during the ninety-day waiting period of our insurance coverage, therefore, we had no insurance. In October 1966, unfortunately we lost the baby boy, William Douglas, during delivery. However, Marilyn once again became pregnant in 1968. I concluded it must be the water in Dallas, because something was happening that did not occur in Utah or anywhere else. Lisa Michelle was born on June 9, 1969, in West Monroe. Marilyn had a c-section with Michelle, so her birth was planned and everything went well. She was a perfect baby girl. We had again been blessed.

During my tenure at Texas Instruments, I designed and constructed a totally new, modern chemical-handling and -processing facility with up-to-date technology. It was quite interesting presenting the new proposed facility to Mark Shepard, Chairman and CEO of Texas Instruments. Mark Shepard was an eccentric individual. Texas Instruments required a casual workplace. Mark carried this to the extreme. His work attire consisted of blue jeans, tee shirt and sneakers with no socks. One leg of his pants was always slightly rolled up. He had a very high opinion of himself and let it be known that he was running every show. I was pleasantly surprised that he approved and complimented me on the chemical plant, the proposal presentation being worth about ten million dollars. It was surprising since he felt chemicals were not critical to the semi-conductor process and used only because they were needed, and not because they were essential to any new development or quality yield. I assumed this was his first exposure to the critical control of chemicals in the electronics manufacturing process. After the presentation, I recall he asked me what I thought of him. I was surprised a CEO would ask such a question. This was in the presence of numerous other Texas Instruments executives. I told him he was exactly what I expected him to be. There were no other questions after that. At that time, Fred Bucy was my supervisor. Bucy later became CEO and Chairman of Texas Instruments.

T.I. was a good place to work and taught me a great deal about management. While at T.I., I completed about forty percent of the hours toward an MBA. T.I. has never had a union, and each year approximately ten percent of its work force (non-performers) are terminated and replaced with new hires. Management has always promoted from within the company. T.I. selects people they believe will have management potential, and sends these selected individuals to numerous management classes and seminars. Fortunately, I was one of those selected.

While at T.I., I received an unsolicited offer to come to Monroe, Louisiana, and be the manufacturing and engineering manager of ITT's micro connector plant (ITT Cannon Electric). This meant a substantial increase in salary and a continual growth up the corporate success ladder. ITT Cannon Electric was a small plant of about four hundred people. I would be one of the two managers reporting to the plant manager. I have no idea how they knew about me. I accepted their offer.

ITT Cannon Electric
Monroe, Louisiana
Manager, Manufacturing and Engineering

In 1968, we moved, against everyone's wishes, especially Mike, from Dallas to Monroe, Louisiana. In 1969, Michelle was born. No further pregnancies occurred after leaving Dallas (different water).

As mentioned earlier, Michelle was born in West Monroe, Louisiana, shortly after our move to Monroe. This left Marilyn with her hands full, i.e., a new baby (Michelle) and Michael, now five years old, who was always going to run away. All this was in addition to getting into a new home and me trying to adapt to a new company. It was difficult, but we made it and did find a home which we enjoyed. One good thing was that we were near Winnfield (via the back roads) so we did a lot of visiting my grandparents and Marilyn's mother and sister Burdette and her family, who lived in Winnfield.

While in Monroe, I had the opportunity to help my grandfather, Pop. In having survey capability, I gathered together some of my fellow employees and did a survey of old property lines around Pop's property. I sent the survey application in to the government for quick claim of the government property. To my surprise, it was approved and he had forty-four more acres of property. Unfortunately, I was not offered any of the land.

Also, while in Monroe, I played music quite often with some of my fellow employees at ITT, and some of the professors at the local college, Northeast Louisiana University, in a band. We had a good time, and enjoyed it, although there was not much pay for our music. I still have some of the old tapes from our music.

While at ITT, I managed all manufacturing and engineering operations. The general manager was Dick Miller. He was a small-stature individual with a strong voice. He believed, as did I, that discipline is the key to profit and growth. We enjoyed Monroe, except for the mosquitoes, humid heat and floods.

ITT Cannon Electric was heavily engaged in the "Man to the Moon" program, supplying parts to NASA and its contractors. The parts we supplied helped put man on the moon, and some of our parts are still on the moon. The manufacture of micro-connectors is heavily manually manufactured. Wires and connectors were assembled under magnifying glass using tweezers—one wire at a time. Over 360 people were used to do the assembly of only a few highly compact connectors. Quality control was essential and critical. Each molded and cast plastic unit, fully assembled had to work. There was no margin for failure or error.

In 1970, ITT began considering moving all operations to Phoenix, Arizona, their headquarters. I was asked to move with the company to Phoenix, but I decided not to move. Some of the individuals I knew at T.I. were at this time now with the Burroughs Corporation in Carlsbad, California. I had received unsolicited offers to come to work as process engineering manager for Burroughs in California. Such a move would not be an increase in management or salary. It was a difficult decision—we decided on California.

In September 1970, we packed up and headed to California—at that time, I recall we had an Oldsmobile Eighty-Eight. Mike was now seven years old and Michelle was a little lady of two years. Therefore, it was a "go a couple hundred miles and stop" type of trip. The air-conditioning would stop working, so we would stop to allow the air-conditioning to cool down enough to start working again. It was hot and the trip took forever. As I recall, although we hated to leave the near-home vicinity, everyone in the family was somewhat excited with the prospects of California. I can still recall today, coming over the last mountain out of the hot desert into the San Diego coastline and the cool breeze that met us. The weather was beautiful (sixty to seventy-six degrees all year around). Also at that time, it was not too heavily populated.

Burroughs Corporation
Carlsbad, California
General Manager, Carlsbad Plants

At that time, the Burroughs Corporation was considered one of IBM's competitors, with IBM being the major company in the electronics industry. Burroughs was primarily into business machines, such as calculators, adding machines, etc. The first computers were being developed during this period. Burroughs' first large computer, developed for the military, engulfed a complete thirty- by fifty-foot room, full of air conditioners to keep it cool.

Plant site, next to Pacific Ocean, photo of myself at Burroughs Corp.

My responsibility was to provide the process, procedures and development of printed circuit boards, semi-conductors and integrated circuits. The boards were made to fit a particular machine and/or computer. They ranged in size from small (one inch by one inch) to large (four feet by four feet). Each was precision drilled, laminated, plated, stuffed and soldered before shipment to the assembly location. The plant was located on the coast next to the Pacific Ocean. One could walk from the building down to the ocean.

We purchased a home in Carlsbad, California, overlooking flower fields of bird of paradise and the ocean, a beautiful view. The houses had little to no insulation, no air-conditioning and only heat. It was interesting to note that the temperature from the coast going inland would either increase (summer) or decrease (winter) approximately one degree Fahrenheit per mile, from a temperature on the coast of approximately sixty-six degrees. In other words, you could basically choose what temperature in which you wanted to live. We lived about one and a half miles from the coast. At that time, our home cost approximately $35,000, which in today's economy would be worth $500,000 to $750,000.

After getting settled in our home, we began to enjoy California. It truly was an excellent place to live. Mike got into motorcycles, as if he was born on one. However, he sincerely disliked school. Marilyn would drive him to school, let him out and he would beat her back home. He finally settled in and it wasn't too bad. Unfortunately, Michelle became Mike's "take it out on her" person, which we had considerable difficulty resolving. All in all, California was a good place to live and work. Everyone enjoyed it. Unfortunately, as with everywhere, when we left California, a lot more people were moving to California. The flower fields were being sold for apartments and crowds were gathering. Even then, it was tough to give up.

Within six months with Burroughs, I had become the manager over all engineering and manufacturing. However, we had a general manager who was not very effective. I had tried to help him put together plans and budgets to improve the plant's performance. He rejected my proposals. I advised him and obtained his permission to forward my proposed plans and budget to corporate headquarters. Within one month, my plans and budget for the plant were accepted by corporate headquarters and I became general manager of the two plants in the area. The former general manager was sent back to Detroit.

These plants I managed were corporate in-house owned and operated facilities. These plants produced the printed circuit boards and integrated circuits for other plants that assembled business machines (adding machines, etc.) for the market. In other words, we produced the components for these machines and eventually the computers. I recall the first business computer manufactured by Burroughs. This computer occupied an approximate thirty-foot by forty-foot room, heavily air-conditioned. This same computer today would fit in one's pocket.

California was an excellent place to live. The weather was incomparable. It seldom rained and stayed between sixty-five and seventy-five degrees all year around, except for approximately one week in September, when the temperature reached 95 to 110 degrees, due to the Santa Anna winds from the desert.

Needless to say, I played a lot of golf. Mike became highly interested in motorcycles (motocross) and dirt bikes. Michelle was still in preschool. Each summer, Mike and I would go camping. One summer we flew in a small airplane into a campsite high in the Sierras. The site was seldom used and was so dirty, we slept outside on the ground rather than the beds. A cloud of dust would occur when the mattress was touched. A lot of memories can be related to our tenure in California.

My Burroughs manufacturing facilities were ultra clean to avoid defects in the integrated circuits. We employed about five hundred people. This was during a period when bomb threats were the going thing. During my tenure as manager, one threat a week for about six months was not uncommon. These threats finally faded away, after numerous precautions were put in place. I had a system installed such that within a few seconds the location of the telephone caller could be determined. After that, the calls stopped.

While in California, I served on various committees, including the planning commission for Carlsbad. We were one of the major employers in the area and therefore, were well received by the city.

After about two years with Burroughs, I received a call one day inviting me to dinner. I had dinner with two individuals, whom I had never met, from Associated Metals, out of New York City. I had assumed they were vendors and were looking for business with us. They made me a generous job offer to manage a tin smelter in Texas City, Texas. I was completely caught off guard and I could not understand why I was offered something so far removed from what I was doing. I advised that any move from my present job would require a contract. They requested I prepare the contract.

I had no desire to leave Burroughs or California; however, I had been advised by the CEO of Burroughs that within the next six months to one year, I would probably be offered a vice president position in Detroit, Michigan (Burroughs' headquarters), and given six to eight plants to oversee and manage. This was a concern, which meant I would probably have to move to Detroit and become a corporate headquarters vice president (married to Burroughs).

Over the next several weeks, I worked on a contract, with very mixed emotions, to go to Texas or Detroit. Within this first contract I had ever prepared, I listed everything one could ever want in a contract—I. e. fivefold increase in salary, perks of all kinds, automobiles, clubs, insurance, job security—on and on. It was one of those deals one would expect to be negotiated or totally rejected. During this interim, Marilyn and I went to see the plant (tin smelter) in Texas City. It reminded me of a bombed-out city, one of the worst facilities I had ever seen. I decided I had no choice but to go to Detroit; however, I decided not to go to Detroit but to seek another job elsewhere.

I met again with the Associated Metals people and handed them the contract. To my surprise, no one read or looked at the contents of the contract, but turned to the approval (last page) area and signed it. I was now in a position where a final decision had to be made by me. I went to see the CEO of Burroughs and showed him the offer and contract. He advised me this was a contract basically no one should reject. He also noted that it would require ten to fifteen years for me to achieve this type of compensation and benefits with Burroughs. He suggested I try it and if it did not work out, my opportunities and position with Burroughs would be available, if I wanted to return.

I advised Associated Metals I would accept the contract (five years) as agreed upon and we headed for Texas.

Gulf Chemical and Metallurgical Co. (GCMC)
Texas City, Texas
Vice President and General Manager

The move from the air-conditioned world of the San Diego area to the humidity and heat of the Houston/Texas City area was quite dramatic. Also, just as dramatic in contrast was moving from the ultra-clean facilities at Burroughs to the dust, dirt, dilapidated buildings and tin smelting furnaces at Texas City. In addition to all this, I worked with an individual (CEO) who had basically no management skills. Therefore, there was a hostile, radical union in place at the tin smelter. After seeing all this, I understood why Associated Metals (owned GCMC) did not read and just signed my contract. My work was cut out for me.

My family and I decided not to live in Texas City and bought a home in Nassau Bay, Texas, about twenty miles from Texas City. This was one of those "I've just got to have this house" by Marilyn. The house was beautiful on the outside, but torn up on the inside. There were holes in the wall, padlocks on doors we could not enter, bad carpet, etc., a totally unattended house. Over the next year, we made the house into a home and have lived there ever since.

The first year at GCMC was a challenge. I brought in management people that had worked with me before and we built a good management team, including the union labor leaders. It became evident we were trying to build a better working environment, improve the facilities and provide an open, above-board relationship with everyone. We also purchased and installed the latest state-of-the-art rotary furnace which replaced seventy-five percent (four) of the brick furnaces (a total of six). The electro-plating facility was refurbished with the latest state-of-the-art equipment, the grounds were cleaned of trash and of environmentally unsafe materials. The overall plant and its operations in general began to be recognized by the city and its employees as a good place to work. Pride in the company became evident with employee picnics, ball and golf teams, etc. We had become a team company, not a plant of union workers and management.

In considering the purchase of the rotary furnace, the engineering manager and I went to Lalea, Sweden, to review and possibly purchase the furnace. This was a steel-producing area and the furnace we were considering was being used to produce steel. Upon arrival to the facility, we were greeted by a lovely blond young lady receptionist. Behind her on the wall was a large photo, approximately two by three feet. It was interesting to note it was a picture of her, nude above the waist. It was something I did not expect, but it did get your attention. My comment to her was "very nice." This was commonplace over there, not much modesty.

**Gulf Chemical and Metallurgical CO, Texas City, TX.
Only tin smelting plant in USA**

Inside smelter building—tin smelting furnaces (four) and holding tanks of molten tin (approximately 700 degrees F.)

Installation of New Kaldo Rotary Furnace

We were treated very nicely by everyone and spent about ten days in Sweden. We purchased the furnace and installed it in the plant. It was a major improvement in production efficiency.

There were some situations which created difficulties. Each month, we received tin ore from Bolivia, South America, which had previously been unloaded from ships by Longshore Union people at Texas City docks. This was extremely costly and very inefficient. I decided to divert the ships to another location and use our people to unload the ships, thereby handling the ore only two times instead of four times, saving approximately one million dollars each year. My plan was met by Longshore Union people threatening death to me and my family. Fortunately, nothing happened and the savings plan worked without difficulty.

Another situation which greatly troubled me was a longtime employee taking advantage of his position and the company's trust in him. This employee had a handicapped child. I made the decision for the company to pay an amount each month for this child's treatment. This occurred over a period of about one year, when I received a call one night from a foreman at the plant. This employee, who was a supervisor, was stealing tin from the company amounting to about $1,000 to $2,000 per week. Once a week, late at night, this man would use two five-gallon steel buckets to dip into molten tin and carry the buckets full of molten tin, weighing about sixty to seventy pounds each, to an area with a hole in the fence and deposit them there. Later, on his way home and after the tin had cooled and was no longer molten, he picked up the containers and thereafter sold the pure tin to scrap dealers. He was terminated without pressing any charges for the theft. It was remarkable he was not killed or maimed from the molten metal, which was approximately 720 degrees F. It is also interesting to note that later, upon applying for another job, he gave me as a reference—he had a weird way of thinking.

Upon my arrival at GCMC, the company had been in operation for about three years. Prior to its start-up, the plant had been idle for about ten to fifteen years. The plant was built by the U.S. Government during the early 1940s to produce tin for the World War II effort. There were and are no tin mines or production facilities in the United States. During World War II, the ships of tin being imported from other countries were being sunk by Germans and/or Japanese. The plant was built on the South Texas coast to allow tin ore to come from South America (primarily Bolivia) into the Gulf of Mexico and be protected from attack. A few years after the war, after the U.S. Government had a stockpile of tin available, the plant was abandoned. Only when the U.S. Government stockpile of tin shrunk to a low level did the smelting of tin become economically feasible. This prompted the purchase of the facility by Associated Metals of New York and the beginning of GCMC. Some five years after my departure, it is also noted that the facility made the list as a major hazardous waste site (caused by the U.S. Government) and once again ceased operations. The site (in 2002) has now been cleaned and all structures removed. The plant no longer exists.

Upon leaving GCMC in 1980, I began looking for other employment opportunities. I received offers of employment from Control Data Corp. to manage a plant in North Carolina, from ITT in Syracuse, New York, from Memorex in California and from the Burroughs Corp., which was now called UNISIS Corp. (Burroughs Corp. merged with the Sperry Corp.), near Boston, Massachusetts. Burroughs people wanted me to return to run a plant there; however, I decided not to move the family. We would stay in Nassau Bay, Texas. I would look for something in the area.

Brief Employment again with Texas Instruments
Stafford, Texas

Although Texas Instruments normally never hires management from outside the company and it had been over ten years since my departure from the company, I called some individuals with whom I had stayed in contact over the years. Within two hours after my call, a job offer in the Houston/Stafford area was made to manage a division of Texas Instruments. The manager of the Texas Instruments operations in the Houston area was a friend with whom I had worked while with T.I. in Dallas, Texas. I accepted the job for substantially less pay and I worked for Texas Instruments at Stafford for approximately four months. Upon my arrival at Texas Instruments, I advised them I was still searching for a company to manage or purchase and hopefully, this job was a temporary situation. My friend understood and said he was pleased to work with me again, if only for a short period of time. Texas Instruments was and is an excellent corporation that has never been unionized. I was employed for about four months before receiving an offer to become president of a local Houston company—Kocide Chemical Corp.

Kocide Chemical Corp.
Almeda Road, Houston, Texas
President

In early 1980, I was contacted by a consultant friend and asked if I would consider running a small company (approximately $3 million to $4 million in sales) called Kocide Chemical Corporation, located here in Houston. The company had outgrown their present president's capability. I interviewed with the board of directors and was offered the position of president to run the company. I accepted and established a salary in excess of my previous salary while at Gulf Chemical and Metallurgical Co. and more importantly, was given an equity position (private stocks) in Kocide with additional stocks depending upon performance of the company.

Kocide Chemical Corp. manufactured copper-related products, the most noted product being an ultra-fine powder of copper oxide that is mixed with water and sprayed on citrus products, nuts, vegetables, coffee, cocoa and trees and shrubs to prevent fungus growth. The people using this product treated the name similar to asking for Coca Cola. It was the premium copper oxide product and carried a premium price of approximately seventy to eighty percent mark-up over cost. This was an excellent cash flow company. Copper oxide is obtained by taking scrap copper (purchased from scrap dealers and copper scrap off the street) at the copper commodity price per pound and dissolving the scrap in acid to make copper sulfate. Then it is filtered and kiln fired to make copper oxide. It is a dusty, smelly and bitter-to-the-taste, hot process. A sure way to stop smoking was to work at Kocide around the copper oxide dust. My son, Mike, worked with me one summer when he was still in high school. It was an experience he still talks about. The temperature that summer was unbearably hot and wearing rubber boots and protective clothing, he realized getting an education was a necessity, in order to keep from having to work in that type of environment. He came from work each day sweaty and covered with blue powder. He was certainly glad when school started.

During my five-year tenure with Kocide, we expanded into additional U.S. markets and, more importantly, became a major international player establishing markets in Africa, South America and Europe. In a three-year period, we grew from $3 million to $4 million in sales to $25 million to $30 million in sales. This required expansion of our plant facilities and pursuit of other manufacturing and distribution locations, including purchasing a copper sulfate manufacturing plant and some copper mining operations in New Mexico, to meet the expanding market.

Kocide Chemical Corp., office building

Working with all the people at Kocide was a memorable experience and gave me many opportunities to visit countries overseas in pursuit of international markets. My experiences included flying on the Concord, spending a night on Mt. Kilamanjaro in Tanzania, Africa, several days in Senigra in Kenya, visiting Italy, France, Sweden, England, the Netherlands, most all of Europe, Brazil, Switzerland and various other foreign countries. Marilyn accompanied me on some of the trips.

I was asked what I liked most about these trips and my answer was always "coming home."

Once, my vice president of marketing and I were in Tanzania near Aresha, where poverty is prevalent everywhere. Dressed in our suits, we were being taxied to the Ministry of Agriculture, where we hoped to sell Kocide 101 for use on coffee and cocoa. Our vehicle malfunctioned and stopped on a road that was isolated, except for African natives in ragged clothes and no shoes, carrying very large machetes. We could only hope for the best when they all gathered around our vehicle. After a short conversation with the driver in their native language, these people descended under the vehicle and repaired the tailpipe, which had fallen off, and reattached it to the vehicle. They asked nothing in return for helping us and their only comments to my vice president and me were "Jambo"(which means "hello"). It goes to show you cannot necessarily judge people by what they may appear to be. They were very friendly.

We visited some of the native villages in Tanzania. The kids kept asking for an object we had. To my surprise, they wanted a simple pencil and were extremely pleased when we passed out pencils.

There were numerous other experiences of interest, which could fill another chapterof this book.

During our search for other possible locations to manufacture or purchase companies that could produce Kocide 101, I contacted the Griffin Corporation in Valdosta, Georgia, which was a company similar in products to Kocide. Rusty Griffin was the owner of the agriculture products company, which had been started by his father.

It became obvious, after a couple of meetings, that the Griffin Corporation was more interested in buying us than us buying them. A deal was struck and we agreed to sell the Kocide Chemical Co. to the Griffin Corporation. This transaction occurred in late 1984. I realized that the vice president of marketing and his people would probably no longer be needed, therefore I contacted some people who were our competitors and who also wanted me to come work with them, managing companies. Through this outside company, I established a marketing division operation in Houston for the Kocide people to run. This now put them in competition with Griffin/Kocide. Nothing in the sale of the company contract prevented me from doing this after the sale transaction of Kocide to Griffin. Part of the transaction deal included the fact that I would continue to operate Kocide until Griffin personnel could take over. I continued for approximately four months after the transaction. As in all transactions of this type where "if it ain't broke, don't fix it," Griffin tried to fix Kocide by letting the marketing staff go, as expected. The Griffin people took over the marketing and Kocide suffered in sales severely with major marketing and profit losses. The Kocide marketing sales people picked up all of these lost Kocide sales areas and also now manufactured a product similar to Kocide in quality.

While at Kocide, I applied for and took the state test and obtained my state professional engineer (P.E.) license. Although I seldom used this P.E. status, it came in handy to stamp off approval of some programs and projects requiring permits by city and/or state. During this period, I also obtained a notary public status, which was also good to have when a notary stamp was necessary in a business or personal transaction.

I left Kocide in mid-1985 and began the pursuit of another company to purchase. Fortunately, the sale left me with sufficient finances to do this from my equity position with Kocide. This was a risk, but, in my judgment, it was a risk worth taking.

During this period after leaving Kocide, I notified acquaintances that I was looking to purchase a small sales-type company ($3. 5 million to $4 million in sales) with approximately two hundred employees. A good candidate company that was brought to my attention was a hose and belt supply and distribution company located inside the 610 Loop here in Houston.

There appeared to be good profit and loss statements and balance sheets showing in excess of $3 million in sales, with approximately thirty percent before-tax profit. I could purchase the company for about six hundred thousand to one million dollars. However, upon an in-depth review, I found an unstated inventory, not on the balance sheet, never taxed, of over one and one half million. This was a disaster waiting to happen if the IRS and/or State of Texas audited this company. They (management) would be put in prison. I continued to search for other opportunities.

An individual, Jay Golding, whom I had met when pursuing the evaluation of companies while at Kocide, called and asked if I would pursue an opportunity with him. I was interested, so we met and reviewed the opportunity.

He was the financial officer with a company in Baytown, Texas, called Hi-Port Industries. Hi-Port Industries was a custom packaging company for the petrochemical and oil companies contract packaging oil, anti-freeze and other auto-related industry products, including some agricultural products.

The principals of Hi-Port, two brothers who founded the company some fifteen to twenty years earlier, wanted to be bought out. Hi-Port was a publicly traded stock on NASDAQ, but basically privately held (no stock available for trading) stock held by these two individuals and was valued at two to three dollars per share (approximately eight hundred thousand) which gave them approximately seventy-five percent ownership of the company.

In reviewing the statements of the company, it became obvious this was an excellent opportunity. In 1983, Hi-Port had suffered a major fire. The plant had been rebuilt with the latest state-of-the-art fully automated packaging equipment and still had capital assets (cash) of over $8 million available after the insurance settlement. In addition, the company had acquired a two percent industrial revenue bond for any other capital that might be required. It was a relatively low-risk, good-possibilities investment.

Hi-Port Industries, Inc.
Baytown/Highlands, Texas
President and C.O.O.

In 1986, Jay Golding and I purchased eighty percent of the two owners' stocks at approximately three dollars per share. Golding owned the majority and would be C.O.O. I purchased the balance for about $208,000 and would be president and C.O.O. We owned majority interest of Hi-Port Industries. The company revenue at this time was approximately $4 million to $5 million per year, with before-tax return of approximately fifteen or twenty percent and approximately $2 million in book asset value.

Jay was one of the best financial people I had ever known. He handled the financial end of the business and I handled the manufacturing, marketing and operational end of the business. We made a good team. During the first two years, we grew the contract packaging business and started manufacturing our own products for industrial and household cleaning and machine lubrication. A plant was purchased in Baton Rouge and a small operational manufacturing facility in Houston. The new product line was called "Chemola." This took the overall business to approximately $8 million revenue per year.

We continued to look and pursue other acquisition opportunities. One day, while reading the *Wall Street Journal*, we noted a possible hostile take-over of a major food distribution conglomerate (a billion-dollar company). By chance, we called the company to see if they might be interested in selling a satellite packaging company they owned called Peterson/Puritan, located in Danville, Illinois. They requested we come to their New Jersey headquarters the next day. We were surprised and shocked with this sudden turn of events, but we were in their offices the next day. They advised they were as surprised with our phone call as we were with them and there was an interest to sell Peterson/Puritan to a qualified buyer. They had no idea who we were, other than they noted our stock traded on NASDAQ. To demonstrate we were sincere, they required us to put up $200,000, not to be returned if we did not or could not financially acquire the company. We did not know and they had not and would not discuss the asking (selling) price of Peterson/Puritan. After careful consideration, we agreed and Jay and I each put up $100,000 and told them "Let's get on with it."

Hi-Port plant complex near Houston handled all phases of bulk storage, custom packaging and warehousing of liquid products. Our quality control and formulated research labs were also located here.

After this, they were very easy to deal with and we developed a good business relationship. In summary, we acquired a contract packaging company with over $50 million in assets with in excess of $130 million in annual revenue with two plants in two states (Illinois and Rhode Island) for approximately $13 million, which was the quick-sale asking sale price of Peterson/Puritan.

We had achieved a major coup. Peterson/Puritan specialized in contract producing and packaging approximately sixty percent of the home, health and body and personal care products such as hair spray, liquids, deodorants, household sprays, etc. in the U.S. This sale and closing occurred within an approximate forty-five-day period from our initial phone call.

Hi-Port had now grown almost overnight from approximately $10 million in revenue per year to over $140 million per year and from 300 employees to over 1,200 employees. We had borrowed a small amount to facilitate the sale, which was paid off within two years.

The Hi-Port stocks on NASDAQ went from approximately five dollars per share to thirty-five to forty dollars per share in a one-month period. It was the fastest-growing stock on NASDAQ for over one quarter.

In1988, the U.S. eliminated trade barriers between Canada and the U.S. A major packaging company in Canada (Continental Can of Canada— C.C.C.) approached us wanting to merge. We stated we would buy them, or they could buy us, but we would not merge. They wanted us more than we wanted them. In 1989, Jay and I and the two brothers sold our stocks to the Canadian company for in excess of forty dollars per share.

I used the funds from the sale to pay off debts (homes in Nassau Bay, Colorado and Lake Livingston) and I still had a considerable amount (greater than one million) to invest or retire on.

After the sale of Hi-Port was completed, I decided to retire. I was fifty-seven years old, still in what I thought was good health with the exception of being overweight, and had received a good pay day. My financial strategy had paid off.

On the day I decided to retire, a friend of mine in commercial real estate wanted me to look at and pursue another company called Barrios Technology, which contracted to NASA and other NASA-related companies, and was located in Clear Lake, Texas. I decided to review Barrios as retirement was getting to be boring.

Barrios Technology
Houston, Texas
Chairman and C.E.O.—Acquired mid-1990

Barrios Technology was a minority-owned company which provided contract services to NASA and other major large companies with NASA contracts.

Barrios had gotten itself in debt when the *Challenger* shuttle disaster occurred and NASA placed a hold on all contracts. Their debt was approximately $500,000 to Texas Commerce Bank and as a result of the type of debt, no other banks or financial institutions would financially help them. They were on the verge of bankruptcy and being taken over by Texas Commerce Bank. This was difficult to understand because Barrios had over $100 million in backlog contracts which they could not honor because they had no cash or cash flow.

I made an offer to purchase the Barrios privately held stock. The offer was rejected by the lady owner (thrown in the waste basket). Without Barrios' knowledge, I then offered to buy the debt from Texas Commerce Bank. They discounted the debt to fifty cents for each dollar. I paid off the debt for approximately $250,000. I now owned Barrios. I advised the Barrios people that I would purchase sixty-six percent stock ownership (controlling interest) for approximately $200,000. The stock had no value at this time, and the company was being taken over by the bank (if I had not bought the debt). The employees agreed and were appreciative to get something for their stocks. The employees, including the previous owner, retained approximately twenty percent of their shares.

Upon becoming CEO, I advised the employees of my plans. We would build and grow the company, and in three to five years, I would try to find a good buyer company to replace me. I did not want my selling the company in three to five years (or anytime) to be a surprise.

I took out a $1 million credit line with a bank and borrowed $500,000 from the bank to place as certificates of deposit to guarantee the credit line. I also pledged a personal guarantee against the certificates of deposit.

Barrios Technology, Inc., corporate headquarters

I then paid myself back from the credit line the amount out of pocket for acquiring Barrios. We then proceeded to honor the over $100 million in backlog contracts. In less than one year, the credit line debt and certificate of deposits debt was honored, Barrios was debt-free and I had two large certificates of deposit.

Barrios grew during my tenure as CEO from approximately $8 million per year and two hundred employees to approximately $20 million per year and close to four hundred employees. It was awarded the highest "quality" contract company award by NASA and was an excellent government contracts service company.

I recognized we could not remain a viable government contract only as a non-minority-owned company and began to pursue commercial (non-government) companies to acquire. I happened to meet people who remembered me from the Burroughs era and Texas Instrument days. One such company, C.D.C. (Control Data Corporation) was most interested in getting into government contracts with NASA. I advised them that Barrios could be a good way to get into NASA. They immediately inquired whether I would consider selling. I played the "I'll think about it" game.

After several discussions, I agreed to sell all Barrios stock of which I owned over sixty-six percent to Control Data Corporation (a Minnesota company) for in excess of $6 million and other considerations. The terms were accepted by C.D.C. The law firm Vinson & Elkins, which we had used previously with the Hi-Port sale, was used by me for the Barrios transaction. Peat, Marwick was Barrios' accounting firm. I was to remain a contract consultant for C.D.C. for one year after the sale at approximately my same salary, and retain the car I had on date of sale (this was how I acquired my first Lexus).

Unfortunately, unknown at the time of the sale, and into the second year (total to be paid over a two-year period) of the sales contract, payment of $2 million by C.D.C., C.D.C. was acquired by another company, who did not want Barrios and tried to renege on the third and final payment. A legal battle ensued and we finally received the final $2 million payment for Barrios.

The Barrios employees with stocks, who had stayed on after I became owner, received a very good payday for their shares of stock. Some were very thankful. The previous lady owner, however, who received the most, has never shown any gratitude for me, without question, saving the company and providing her enough money to retire.

The company that acquired C.D.C. made arrangements by some non-available, highly questionable terms to return Barrios ownership to a woman who had been acting as president of Barrios for C.D.C. after the sale. She was a vice president in my organization and a very capable individual. The terms of this transaction are unknown. Barrios is presently operating and doing well as a minority-owned company, contracting as before to NASA and other major companies in the NASA area. In a period of less than two years (19 months), I bought and sold Barrios for a considerable monetary gain.

H.R.B. Equities, Inc. Investment/Consulting, Houston, Texas
President and C.E.O., owner of Airport Marine (boat Business) Seabrook, Beaumont, & Houston, Texas 1991-1993

During my tenure with Barrios, I loaned money to and became involved with a boat company in Beaumont, Texas, called Airport Marine. On the surface, it appeared to be a good company with in excess of $10 million per year in boat sales and service. Unfortunately, it was not what it appeared to be. It was run by some first-class crooks and was deep in debt. Unfortunately, this was a company I had no interest in buying, and was only trying to help, and therefore, did not do my homework.

All of this resulted from the purchase of a sleek twenty-six-foot boat for Mike, which we now, after the fact, classify as the one-million-dollar boat.

After the sale of Barrios, my attention turned to getting my loaned money back. When it was evident my investment of approximately $200,000 was not going to be repaid, I took over Airport Marine, taking all their assets and legally forming a new corporation with the same name, which was a mistake, and trying to avoid having to clear their debts in order for the new companies to do business. Because of the same name, the vendor companies had a difficult time understanding we did not owe them money, and therefore, would not supply us products to do business. After about a year and an investment of an additional several hundred thousand dollars, it became evident this was not going to work. The marine (boat) industry is operated on a low-integrity basis. The manufacturer financed companies, which I rank lower than the worst used car business. No one could be trusted. I had hoped this might be a good business for Mike and Michelle. However, the interest was not there and it was a mistake on my part.

During my two and one half years (1990-1993) in this boat business, through my investment company (H. R. B. Equities) I acquired the building and land on Nasa Road 1 in Seabrook, Texas. This property had been attained through bankruptcy by the bank I was using. I acquired two buildings and 2.5 acres of land for approximately $250,000. Another $50,000 was put into improvements. The property was leased by H. R. B. Equities to Airport Marine. In 1993, I dissolved and bankrupted all the companies of Airport Marine and declared a taxable loss of in excess of $1 million. The IRS returned approximately seventy percent of my Airport Marine investment, leaving me with a net loss of less than $100,000. Legal suits against the boat suppliers returned me additionally in excess of $300,000. As a result of these actions, the boat business become an unpleasant experience, rather than a major financial loss.

Since that time, over the next ten years, the following has occurred:

Approximately one acre of land and an office building was sold to Lakewood Yacht Club, which paid for a great part of my investment. An approximate ten-foot strip of land along NASA Road 1 was sold to the state of Texas for over $200,000, from which $60,000 was used to construct a new building. The property had paid for itself, plus a sizable profit, through these transactions.

Since 1994, about seventy percent of the building has been leased to Tops-N-Towers (aluminum fabricators) for a continued good return on the investment over the years. It is presently leased for five more years at over $7,000 per month Unknown at the time, but purchased at a good price, the building and land have turned out to be an excellent investment.

Airport Marine was a judgment mistake, however, the results were not financially bad as the building and land today is valued in excess of $1 million with annual rental income of $80,000 to $90,000 per year and all debt free. In hindsight, the boat business worked out rather well financially.

HRB Equities Building, Seabrook, Texas. Now leased to Tops-N-Towers

Chapter 6
Personal Comments

During these past ten to twelve years, there have been some health concerns. In 1993, during all the difficulty with Airport Marine, I had to have some heart-related arteries cleaned out. During the same year (1993), my gall bladder required removal.

Everything went well until 2005 when chest pains reoccurred, requiring more artery cleaning and finally, heart bypass surgery. Also in 2006, the old 1954 knee hurt while I was in the Army, required surgery. Health wise, 1993 and 2005 were not good years.

Now, at seventy-four years of age, health wise everything appears to be functioning well. As the heart doctor says "good for another twenty years."

In ending these chapters about my personal and professional life, I can truly say I have been blessed. I have had a good, long married life (fifty years) with the same wonderful woman. Our children have been everything one could hope for and now we stay young trying to keep up with and spoil six grandchildren (two girls and four boys—two to ten years of age). They make it all worthwhile. We have also been blessed with good business decisions, which have placed us in a category (level) financially I would never have believed as a young professional, that I could achieve.

In regard to family events during my professional life, while I was with the Burroughs Corp. in California, the death of my grandfather occurred. This was complicated by a family conflict, which I still do not understand. My grandfather (Papa), who raised me, knew I could survey. I had earlier done a quick claim for him which added over forty acres to his property. He asked and I complied, to survey out his property (homesite) into eight equal parcels for his living children (neither my brother nor I were included). I completed this survey. He had each member of the family draw the eight parcels from a hat.

Everyone accepted the land parcel they had drawn. He also suggested they swap if they wanted to do so. This occurred about three years prior to his death.

Upon his death, four of the family members sued for invalidation of his will and the method by which the parcels were obtained, claiming he was incompetent at the time. I entered the suit with my own attorney and prevailed in having the suit dismissed. This action split the family apart and to this date and to their death, would not and will not associate with one another. Some have once again accepted me and agree they were wrong in their actions. Little things in a family can sometimes have big, lasting negative effects that cannot be understood. The important thing is to never let this type situation happen again.

Chapter 7
My Music

I also cannot complete this autobiography without some comment about my music.

I was raised listening to gospel music. My grandmother, who raised me, could play several instruments (mostly guitar and piano) by ear. I became self-taught on how to play one chord at a time on the guitar. Finally, I caught on as far as what to do, when to do it and which chord sounded right. I can truthfully say the first time I tried to play the harmonica, I could play a tune, a note at a time. This surprised me. From there, it became easy for me to play. I learned to play other instruments simply by trial and error and/or getting a book which listed the chords with each song. After that, it was just a matter of listening to a tune and finding the right chord in which the song was being played, begin playing along or playing the song.

I began trying to blend together all the instruments I could "halfway" play and record several instruments as a band. My interest in music began basically quite late in life after I retired from my professional life and had time and money to buy equipment for recording purposes. Needless to say, my singing was not good, therefore, most of my earlier recordings were all instrumental. I started by recording on an old reel to reel, playing harmonica and guitar together, then recording this on a cassette tape, then recording the cassette back onto the reel to reel, then back to the cassette, each time adding another instrument. This took a long time with no room for error and very poor recording quality.

I finally decided to quit or buy something better. In 1989, I purchased a four-track cassette recorder. I was now in business. Finally, I purchased a six-track recorder and CD burner. This equipment is what I have today.

Beginning in 1990, I decided to write and record some of my own songs. Since then, I have written and recorded about forty to forty-five of my songs.

If I had the concept of the song on my mind, I found I could write the lyrics in about thirty to forty-five minutes and record it to my music within the next couple of hours.

Normally, it takes about two to three hours for me to record a song involving four to five instruments, during which time I may use different instruments and different blends and sounds to get what I consider the best results, or what I conceive to be the best sound (vocal included, which isn't good, but I've got to sing).

To date (2006), I have recorded over 200 songs. This translates to over 600 to 800 man-hours. After my heart operation in 2005, the first three fingers of my left hand have become numb or sometimes quite sensitive. This means playing the guitar becomes limited. Therefore, my recordings have somewhat stopped. It isn't as enjoyable as it used to be.

My recordings were made, generally, late at night when there were no telephone interruptions, in a quiet corner of my house.

We'll see what the future brings in this area of my life.

2005 Family Photos

Chapter 8
Professional Management Advice

I have also been asked by professionals at universities and companies where I have given speeches to write a book on my professional experience. Unfortunately, I could not think of enough things in this area to fill a book. I contend, if one succeeds in their objectives, it could probably be summarized in a chapter or less. I have offered some comments toward these questions in this document.

The question of how does one go about buying a company and/or succeed in management is difficult to answer. This question occurs most often when I am giving a talk to professionals on business or addressing graduate and/or undergraduate students. I try to advise as follows:

There are numerous books on management, positive thinking, guidelines that have fancy titles for management and other discussions and descriptions on these subjects. Some of these may help or some may confuse. I have never put much stock in these books because every situation and its makeup of people (attitudes, personalities, capabilities, etc.) is different. The guidelines may be useful, but the application is what you make it. You must understand the work environment you are in and based upon this environment, find methods or ways to improve it. Unexpected tasks and contributions by you can become a valuable stepping stone on the ladder of becoming successful toward your objectives. However, one should always follow the guidelines and structure of the company in pursuing your objectives.

DO NOT use the word "CAN'T." This is very important. Strike it from your vocabulary. Everyone can, if they set their mind to it. As a manager, I would insist that those who work with me not use the word "can't."

One must take what is available to him at any given time and hopefully, make the best decision he can on what to do and upon what you know and what you want. In most every situation, there is a risk; sometimes one risk is greater than another. If one cannot accept and take the risk, then one should not proceed. This has to do with the confidence placed in yourself, what you hope to achieve and the assets and capability which you deem you have to achieve your goal. If any of these assets are questionable, making something of them can become difficult. In other words, confidence, absent of doubt, is a very important ingredient on the road to success.

Look for opportunities inside and outside your working area. If a professional opportunity for growth presents itself, go for it. There is no textbook answer on how to do this. You must be prepared to fulfill what you are seeking. There is no room for doubt or failure in pursuit of your objectives. Learn from any failure that may occur as a "what not to do."

In your growth stages, capability and knowledge are much more important than money. As you grow in the ranks, the money will take care of itself. In my career, I have taken positions of less money and title first to acquire the knowledge of the job.

Do not be an ego seeker. Titles mean very little, except looking good on a business card. Egos have never acquired a single thing that's worth anything. It may make you feel good and big, but at the same time, it can get you destroyed. Forget ego and pursue tangible things.

In my situation, I changed jobs approximately five times before becoming general manager of a company. In each different company, I had a different responsibility than the previous company. This meant I had held just about every job position available within a commercial marketing manufacturing company, including research, marketing, sales, manufacturing, quality control, process engineering and accounting. In other words, I was experienced and familiar with every aspect of the company. This is important, but not absolutely necessary in order to manage a company. If I had not been confident I could handle the challenge, the opportunity would have passed me by, the risk too great. We are back to never considering the word "CAN'T." Be confident in yourself, be prepared because the opportunities are always there. You just have to look for them and pursue them.

I had a basic concept in managing. A manager or leader "manages people," not machinery or operations. You work with people. They may report to you, but it is critical they work with you and you with them. They don't work for you, they work with you. They become an extension of you and you of them, from the line operator or janitor, to the supervisors, managers and vice presidents of the company. This is probably the most critical element of being successful in a company. Share the opportunities and responsibilities with them as well as difficulties. Do not be afraid to delegate and show respect for their capability. A good group of people will pull the company and you through growth and hard times. If you are not one of them, on their level, it will be difficult. Try to know them well enough on a personal level and be sincere with people. If you are not sincere in these endeavors, the people will know and any respect of you or for you will be gone. You cannot pretend, they will see through you. Pedestal sitters and ego seekers are destined for failure. This is very important in your growth within a company and the success of the company. Products are what you sell, the people that make these products and sell these products make or break the company.

Don't give excuses, be definitive and decisive in your answers and questions. Define what you can do, not what you "can't do."

This is probably the most important element of management and growth you will encounter and have to master to continue growing.

In summary, things to remember for growth:

- Avoid the cant's.
- Don't be an ego seeker
- Be a leader, working as a team, share information and responsibilities.
- Excuses of "don't have time," "not enough people" are to be avoided.
- Be a decision maker with definitive answers. Do not, as I call it, "hem haw" around an answer.
- Never start a program you do not plan to continue.
- Be grateful for what you have received—it may have to be stopped.
- Positive workers and thinkers generally are successful and motivated.
- A definition of goals, objectives and the path to achieve are essential in management and professional growth. Always believe you can and must make it work.
- Always try to do more than is expected of you as this will define you as a leader, not a follower.
- You'll know if you "can or don't want to."

Chapter 9
Buying/Selling Companies

What does one look for if trying to buy a company or start a business? Numerous things must be considered. A few are listed below:

- What is the financial history of company or business?
- What types of people are involved? Can they work as a team with you? If you have a history with companies, this becomes less important because you will have people in previous companies from which you can draw.
- What are the plans and budget for the company? How have they performed against these in the past?
- Can you meet the financial sale price of the company and is it a fair number?
- Can you meet the challenge (know how) to make it grow?
- Could you sell it, if desired, in the next few years?
- What are the downside risks? List in order of importance and financial impact. Have an answer of what to do for each one.
- Define, if possible, all assets available to work with for growth and profitability. What, if any, are hidden assets?
- To purchase assets or stock in a company, first you must have a financial base, either through borrowing money, having equity to use, have an investment backer (who believes in you) or some other financial assets (could be part of equity) you can use.

In my case, I built an equity base within a company, as part of my agreement to become president of the company. If the company is successful, your equity grows.

The question becomes "How do you get to be president or get to the point that some company wants you to be president or manager?" Your performance as a professional will determine this factor. If you perform and contribute above the norm, your potential will be noticed. If you follow the standard routine, that's normally where you will stay. If you cannot recognize what requires or allows you to be above the norm, or greater than the routine job description, you probably will be passed over next promotion time. Hopefully, you can see or conceive things that others cannot and promote your ideas. In other words, do things both expected and greater than expected of you—in and outside your work place.

Most important, what assets are available or can be made available to work with? For example, Hi-Port (which I bought into) had $8 million in the bank with a two percent industrial loan and all new equipment, which was an excellent asset base with relatively low risk. Barrios (another company I acquired) had over $100 million in back-log government contracts and an excellent professional group of people, which was another very low risk.

The high risk comes when a growth potential asset cannot be clearly defined or is not evident. This means you are working with only the history of the company, which can or may change in a very short period. In this situation, the people and their capabilities available become very important.

In the final analysis, I try to follow my "gut" feeling about buying, selling or pursuing an objective. There are no "sure things," only potentials or possible opportunities. Make the most of each one, but always remember, credibility and integrity are the greatest assets you can possess. However, do not assume when pursuing an opportunity that everyone is credible. Be careful in evaluating the person with whom you are negotiating. Make decisions based upon facts or tangible items, not just because "someone said it's so." Gain sufficient knowledge or capability, such that when you ask a question, you already know the answer.

When I asked myself what was the most important or major factor that helped me proceed to the next level of professional growth, the answer was always the same. Either I knew someone or someone knew me or enough about me and my professional experience, and it assisted me toward my next management level. If I had been a follower or just did exactly what I was told to do rather than being an innovator and/or motivator, recognition for growth would not have occurred.

Get to know and work with and around individuals you respect, learn from them, assist them in their growth and you will be recognized for your growth potential. Look for ways to improve your job and contribute to your work place. Don't try to achieve more than your capability. A failure is an experience that is hard to overcome. As you grow, always remember, the people around you put you there and they can also bring you down. If you can't handle the job, explain your difficulties. Good managers want you to grow and will assist you in being better prepared or find a position better suited for you. Don't let the job drag you down.

I have a saying which I advise young people beginning their careers— "Don't build yourself into a box." This means, don't do things financially you may want, or would like to do, because you now financially can. In other words, don't go buy a big, expensive house because you now can—this is "building your box." One never knows what tomorrow may bring. Always plan for the down side; the up side will take care of itself. This is a personal discipline. It can also apply to your professional character.

Selling a Company

I have been involved in the selling of three companies. The methods I used when I wanted to sell were as follows:

- Decide what you feel the company is worth—this value may change depending upon the possible buyer and unexpected situations. Value could go up or down.
- Be prepared to justify your position and asking value, i.e. , put yourself as the buyer rather than the seller—identify good, strong and weak areas.
- Spread the word through contacts of your interest to sell, particularly if you know who might be interested in your company. I call it "throwing out the bait."
- Value may go up or down, based upon this interest level. For example, I found someone who wanted to get involved with NASA when I had Barrios. This was an excellent interest contact. The result was that I acquired Barrios with the intent to sell in three to five years. After less than three years, I had an opportunity to meet this objective. The strategy then became "how can I make the most of this opportunity and not lose it."
- Prepare the company and your team of people for the sale. This

may be the most difficult part of the transaction. The people must want the sale to occur if you want to achieve the best value. I always considered, "How will this affect the employees"– their best interest must come first.

- Obtain good audit people and make certain the books are accurate and up-to-date. Be able to, or have someone capable of, explaining every phase of what you and/or the company are doing, and plan to do in the future.

- Share your plans, budgets and optimistic forecast for the company. If not available, get busy. Be prepared to defend— test it with your people—they must be involved. A positive presentation makes the price look better.

- It must be, as I say, "a good dog-and-pony show."

Fortunately, I have been very successful in all my selling attempts. In the beginning, I advised the people in companies I acquired that I planned to invest and grow the company and would be trying to sell in three to four years, or shorter, if a good buyer for the company came along. If everyone helped do this, everyone would benefit (financially, or through employment tenure). It worked and everyone has benefited.

Fortunately, I am now in a position to buy or live most anywhere I would like. However, I like where I am and don't need the box to get any bigger.

Hopefully, some of these suggestions will be remembered and assist young professionals in their growth.

I have been asked, "What is wealthy?" and "Are you wealthy?" My answer has always been, rather than give financial or tangible values, I suggest the following as a definition of wealth. Wealth is when one has reached a financial level in their life when they can buy what they want, when they want and how they want, without it having a noticeable or measurable negative effect or impact on their financial net worth or standard of living. I try to live by this definition.

Stay positive, set high goals and make it happen—you can!!!

About the Author

Ray Barrett was born in Georgetown, Louisiana, in 1932, during the Great Depression. Ray's dad died at an early age, leaving him and a younger (baby) brother with basically no means of support. It was debated that they should be put in an orphanage. Ray and his brother went to live with their mother's parents. Ray resided with his grandparents until, at the age of eighteen, he left to work and live on his own.

The author faced many hardships in his struggle to succeed. He had little education and no money. Jobs were hard to find, and those that were available required guts and a sincere need to continue on the job.

This is a document of determination and an individual striving to succeed, progressing from basically zero assets to a financially independent status at retirement. It also suggests what is necessary for one to progress professionally to achieve a financially independent status.

During the last twenty years of his career Ray was the CEO and owner of three corporations, which he personally purchased, operated, and within three to five years sold to other companies, which led to his financially independent retirement. As Ray might say, it may not be easy, but it can be done.